1

BROWN GAL'S RISING

BY
CECELIA ANTOINETTE
ORIGINAL C. 1984

Glover Lane Press
Publishers Since January 2000
4570 Van Nuys Blvd Suite 573
Sherman Oaks, CA 91403
gloverlanepress@gmail.com
www.gloverlanepress.webs.com

Images Provided by CeCelia Antoinette
Book Cover Design: Azaan Kamau
ISBN-13:978-0615574790
ISBN-10:0615574793
The Mission of Glover Lane Press is to Uplift, Empower, Elevate
the Masses and Provide American Jobs. Every book published by
Glover Lane Press and it's many imprints, is printed and
manufactured in the United States of America, ensuring and
maintaining American employment.

DEDICATION

BROWN GAL'S RISING is dedicated to
my Mother, **Naomi M. Bruton,**
my big Sister, **Laura K. Bruton,**
my Grandmother, **Princella Hartman**
(who at printing is 106 years old),
my Self **CeCelia Antoinette** (Bruton)
my Sisters of the Goddess/Feminist
Divine "Movement" Continuum,
and girls and women of All Colors, Races,
Planets
and All who have dared to meet
themselves and become...
Rise!!!

SPECIAL THANKS and ACKNOWLEDGEMENTS

First Reading Cast & Frank Silvera
Writers Workshop
Mizan Nunes
Phyllis Yvonne Stickney
Cheryl Lane-Lewis
Debra Vanardo
Lavora Grant
Pat White, Director

Theatre 22, Blue Diamond Productions
and First Performance Cast
Renee Joshua-Porter (and Milani)
Curtiss I. Cooke'
Renee Flemings
Kathi Bentley
Denise Kennedy
Jeffrey "Wayne" Miller, Producer &
Assistant Director

Brooklyn College Cast and Patrick Coker
Renee Joshua-Porter
Renee Flemings
Terry Wyche'
Geany Masai
Therese Coleman

Under One Roof Cast and Wickham Boyle
& Cheryl
Richarda Abrams

Paulette Lunn
Cherise Trahan
Robert Evans
Nicole Ari Parker
Miche Braden-music, Afia-percussion,
Candace-choreography

Naomi, Laura, Cecil, Cicero I & II, Quica &
PLUMEings Productions, Gloria Lynch-
Boone, Jane Galvin-Lewis, Spencer Barros,
Curtis II, JD & Dolly, Jackie Greene, George
Lamboy, Arthur French, Melissa Maxwell,
Marcia Lowry, and Mylika Davis

And a heartfelt and profound thank you to
PHYLLIS HYMAN for taking the stage with
BROWN GAL'S RISING and giving one of
my songs wings...

Contents

Foreword - a Poem
By Irma P. Hall

*I was honored and a bit intimidated when asked to
write a foreword for my God-Child's project! I
watched this brown girl/ woman-child grow into
womanhood and have constantly been amazed at her
artistry and courage.* To me she is the essence
of
EBONINITY

For a Brown Gal Rising
I am the Nubian Queen. Lustily swinging
my hips,
Down into Egypt's land,
Gliding through the land of the Israelite,
Sailing my barge to check out Rome,
Sending a whisper through a thousand years,
To Picasso.
That he really should check me out.
And he did,

I am the Black Madonna,
Finding no room at the inn,
On the journey to the land of the free,
in chains.
My beauty and majesty so overwhelming to
my captors,
They built me a myth.
My strength so formidable,
I had to survive.
And I did.

I am the sassy sister.

11

Got my own pad,
My own bread, my own elevator,
To my own star.
My mind clicking so fast
It shames computers
So Hot,
They had to open doors
Close mouths, shift minds
And watch my smoke.
And they did.

Irma P. Hall

Me and My Brown Gal 20 Years Later

By Renee Joshua-Porter

In retrospect, I can now see how the play
BROWN GAL'S RISING was given to me
at a divinely pivotal time of my life. Newly
married, very pregnant, stubborn and
determined to continue to do this thing of
theater, wife, and nurturer of inner and outer
self, I was so scared and confused. The
repeated question of "Where's my pretty
brown gal?" resonated inside of me and the
infant girl would leap" inutero" during
performances-- "Here I am". Confused,
excited, frightened, insecure, proud,
embarrassed, I struggled with fleeting
thoughts of, "They're not talking to you
baby girl, they're talking to me. I'm the
pretty brown gal?! Right? Or am I not? Can
I be her and you be her too? The play
helped me to address on all levels. As I

13

recognize you brown gal, do I emerge equivalent or does your arrival mean my departure?

I found out through the years that measurement was not even necessary. Every tree bears fruit after its own kind and BROWN GAL'S said it best, "Guard your seed!" Although it was talking to the brothers, I have rehearsed, recounted, engraved, and branded that line from that play into every fiber of my life. That baby girl was the first of three seeds that I was honored enough to be entrusted with. As the Executive Director of a nonprofit organization The Burning Bush Family Foundation Inc., I provide educational and recreational programs for children and families and that has been a big and rewarding crop to harvest. I have tried to guard my brown gal, her brothers and others with my life, my words, my prayers and my actions.

Milani Renee Porter has evolved into a bright, very unique young woman. We share a lot of the same artistic genetics but she surpasses me by far with a passion for writing, performing and an early understanding of the beauty in black women. She is always reading about "us" and our hair, our ideas, how misunderstood and under recognized our beauty is in

America. She studied two years overseas in Switzerland, travelling the world and created a blog about being a black woman abroad. Currently, a senior in Washington DC at American University, she is majoring in Journalism with a minor in Multiethnic Studies. Thanks to a great theatrical head start, she is definitely evolving into a **brown gal on the rise.**

Production History:

05/1991- **Theatre 22, NYC**
12/1991- **Brooklyn College, Bklyn, NY**
06/1993 - **Under One Roof, NYC**

SETTING: the bathroom and "living" room of CELESTE, a woman of African-American descent. She is preparing a ritual birthday bubble bath for herself. This play/choreo-poem takes place in her mind as she greets and embraces the different aspects of herself. It really is the left corner, left side of the right mind where all **brown gal's** meet themselves—if we are going to.

PREMISE: **Brown Gal's** who meet and greet themselves can rise.

CHARACTERS / ASPECTS

CELESTE: the woman; the Brown Gal of the play—the Feminine Devine part of the female. The others are aspects of her.

CISSY: the youthful one; the inner child in you; the holder of younger memories for CELESTE.

JO: the robust one; the strength in you; the holder of morality of the Masculine Devine in CELESTE.

BUBU: the black one; the political revolutionary in you; the "Angela Davis" of CELESTE.

EVE: the mysterious one; the consciousness in you; the emerging and constantly evolving consciousness of CELESTE.

BROWN GAL'S RISING
The Production

PROLOGUE

I. EMERGING
In the depths of Me
We were One
Oozing from my pores
From the liquid pool
I can feel my feet

II. GROWTH
Know how I got here
Born a black baby
R-E-S-P-E-C-T
Be a man someday

III. PRETTY BROWN GAL
Where's My Pretty Brown
Gal
Pretty Brown Gal Rap

IV. HATS
I know why
The Hats

PROLOGUE

CELESTE

Daydreaming and I'm thinking of you…

Daydreaming and I'm thinking of you…

Daydreaming and I'm thinking of you…

Look at my mind—

Blowing away…

I. EMERGING

CELESTE

(Assumes the Supreme-esque position)

Really, I'm like any other woman.
I bleed.

I need.

I laugh.

I cry.

I love.

And I long for loving too.

*(Preparing her ritual bubble bath, a heart
beat can be heard faintly in the background)*

CISSY

*(reveals herself, and delicately enters the
tub/circle and plays with CELESTE as they
bathe)*

In the depths of me lives a child.

The child I was.

The child I am.

The child I will be...

sometimes.

The playful one...

The curious one...

The spiteful one—

who doesn't like to be hurt!

Inside of me dwells a child,

Beating—

beating fiercely—

To be set free.

In my smile,
My child is emerging.
Call me Cissy.

CELESTE/ OTHERS
(as a whispered echo)
Cissy...   Cissy... Cissy...

JO
(reveals self, muscularly)
We were one at one time—ONE!
Male and Female—ONE!
Then the sun--
or something ...
Cooked us apart
And made TWO hearts
 beat separately.
His—like strong.
Hers—like weak.
But the strength you see

Is the man-thing in me

Emerging.

Emerging!

Call me JO!

CELESTE/ OTHERS
(as a whispered echo)
Jo… Jo… Jo…

CISSY
The smile…

JO
The man-thing…

CISSY
The child…

CISSY & JO
Emerging… emerging…

*(**JO** and **CISSY** continue their individual actions)*

BUBU
(Rhythmic revelation of self)
Oozing from my pores are
 big, fat, black drops
Of hard earned sweat!
Wet!
Shining back at black me.
Emerging…
Like coal in blue-black Africa
Takes time to become diamonds,
My mind takes time
To become black me.

BUBU & CISSY & JO
But we are surely emerging!

BUBU
From the bottom of a fermenting pit
Comes a drum song beating through…

The rhythm is

the black in me surging!

Call me Bubu!

CELESTE/ OTHERS

(*as a whispered echo*)

Bubu… Bubu… Bubu…

Emerging… emerging!

*(**CISSY, JO** and **BUBU** continue their
actions)*

CELESTE

(Reveals self as if a woman in labor)

From the liquid pool of a mother's womb,

bearing a womb with a pool for others,

the woman in me is emerging.

Bursting surface membranes,

Fragile by definition—

if not by function—

Reaching with searching fingertips…

Up…

Toward a new type of "woman-standing"

Which is not "under-standing" at all.

The woman I see

is the woman in me

Emerging!

Call me Celeste!

CELESTE/ OTHERS

(As an echo)

Celeste… Celeste…Celeste….

Emerging…

Emerging…

Emerging…

Coming up for air!

For there will WE be…

CELESTE

The woman I see…

BUBU

Black as I'm 'sposed to be…

JO

The man-thing in me…

CISSY

The Child in my smile…

CELESTE/ OTHERS

Emerged…

All merged…

All merged….

(BUBU, JO, CISSY continue their actions.
CELESTE prepares to leave tub.)

EVE

(Spiritually revealing self)

I can feel my feet

So close to the ground…

And yet so far away.

I feel the strength…*(pointing, empowering*

JO)

The power…*(pointing, empowering **BUBU**)*

The need …*(pointing, empowering*

CELESTE)

The urge …*(pointing, empowering **CISSY**)*

To stand tall,

Strong,

Independent!

All on my own.

Wanting and needing many things

Then finding them for myself

Makes me feel my own strength

Surging from within.

Call me EVE!

CELESTE/ OTHERS

(as whispered echoes crescendos to a
gradual shout)

Eve… Eve… Eve….

*(**CELESTE** takes towel and steps outside of tub/circle)*

II.   GROWTH

(CELESTE/ OTHERS take to their feet as they "grow" [goes to dresser] gets lotion to anoint herself)

CISSY

Do you know how I got here?

I got here because my Mama and Daddy

Decided to love one another.

They decided – after love—

That they wanted to be partners.

They decided

 that it was worth their time

To have brown [black] babies

And to raise a brown [black] family.

They decided

To pass the names of two families

And the "His-story" of two families

Through rich red [black] blood

And through young black mouths.

I am part of that decision.

BUBU
Well, I was born a black baby
In a white baby world.
No spoon in my mouth.
No shirt on my back.
No swatling to wrap my naked black self.
Little did I know I was inheriting
The dominant genes of Blackness
And all the shades of gray that come with
them.

CELESTE
*(Anointing her thighs, and playing "ring-
around-the roses" as the others try to keep
her out of the circle)*
Girls,
Keep your dresses down
And your pants [panties] up
And your eyes open
If you are gonna keep up with those boys

You are messing with.

I done told you

they ain't no good!

The minute they have their way with you

They are gonna drop you like a hot potato.

And who is gonna respect you then?!

(ala Aretha Franklin)

R – E – S – P – E – C – T

Find out what it means to me….

ALL

R- E- S- P- E- C- T… take care   T- C- B!!!

Respect—just a little bit…

Respect!

CELESTE

Remember that girls?

Well, we all learned respect

When we learned the meaning of that…

Keep your dresses down!

Keep your pants [panties] up!

But we were older and wiser

And giving our daughters the same lines

When we really knew what that meant.

So, how do we change "his"-story?

How do we heed Mama's age-old advice?

How do little girls and grown woman get
respect?

ALL

Re... Re... Re ... Respect!

Find out what it means to me.

Re.... Re... Re... Respect

Find out what it means to me.

Re... re... re... respect.

Find out what it means to me.

Take care T-C- B-

Aww... a little respect...

Ohh... a little respect...

Re... re... re... re....re...re...re...re..

SPECT!!!!

JO

(sung acapella)

Little boy, be a man some day.

Don't run away from responsibility.

See, it's the little things you do

That you may not want to

That will make all the difference in you.

We should take our sons [CELESTE:
daughters...]

Our brothers ...[CELESTE: sisters...]

Our fathers ...[CELESTE: mothers...]

Our uncles ...[CELESTE: aunts...]

Our cousins ...[CELESTE: "cousin-
ettes"...]

Our nephews ... [CELESTE: nieces...]

Our in-laws ...[CELESTE: in-laws...]

Our lovers ...[CELESTE: lovers...]

Aside and say

Little boy, be a man [CELESTE: woman]
someday.

Don't run away from responsibility.
See, it's the little things you do
That you may not want to
That will make all the difference in you.

So just face tomorrow willing to try,
Though sometimes you cry.
Your emotions make you my
little man.
Don't let life get you down
Or your peers make you a clown.
Be the talk of the town!
Be a Man!!!

Take a stand!
Believe that you can!
Because if you try
ALL the powers on High
Will lend a hand.
So, be a Man!

See, it's the little things you do

That you may not want to

That will make all the difference in you--

For me.

III. <u>PRETTY BROWN GAL</u>

EVE
(In the voice of Aunt Sarah)
Where's my **pretty brown gal?**
Where's my **pretty brown gal**?
Where's my **pretty brown gal**...?

CISSY
(Hearing Aunt Sarah and hiding)
Aunt Sarah would call after me
To let me know she was at our house for a visit.
I would hide sometime and not come out right away
Just to see if she would call me.
Then I'd hear...

EVE

Where's my **pretty brown gal**?

CISSY
And I'd come running out
And hug her neck, [they "air" hug]
Playing like she had just gotten there.
She felt so good to me.

Aunt Sarah and her "**brown gal**"….
She was a **brown gal** too—
 now that I think about it.
Kinda like me.
Wonder if somebody called her that
when she was a little girl…
Or if it was something she made up
Just for me.

She had this old wooden wall phone
With the receiver you would hold to your
ear (mock this)
And the dial you had to crank to get the
operator…(crank)

And the operator would answer…

BUBU
(as operator)
Operator…

CISSY
(pleasantly surprised)
and have to dial your calls.
I was taken with that phone.

Well, Aunt Sarah had a stroke
And I would go over to care for her.

*[**JO** becomes "Uncle James" and helps
"Aunt Sarah, **EVE**, to her bed.]*

We would play cards *(mock)*
And dominoes *(mock)*
And I would sneak and let her have a puff
on a cigarette. *(mock)*
That felt good to her.

Mama say….

CELESTE

(as Mama)

"If you be good to Aunt Sarah

she will probably leave you that phone"…

CISSY

I stopped going by so much after that…

Because I wanted to be good to Aunt Sarah

 because I wanted to—

Nothing else.

No matter how crazy I was about that phone.

Aunt Sarah died four years later—

To the date—

From when she had her stroke.

She didn't leave me that phone…

BUBU

(as operator)

click!…

CISSY

[OTHERS assemble in church as pall bearers]

But Aunt Sarah left me something much more.

She left me a good feeling about **BROWN GALS**—

Like her and like me.

I can still hear her calling …

CISSY/ EVE

"Where's my pretty **Brown Gal**?"

BUBU

(stops the revelry with the Pretty Brown Gal Rap)

Huh, pretty brown gal…

Pretty brown gal…

(Brown Gal Rap)

Well, this ain't no place
 for a **pretty brown gal**
of royal African blood
To not realize her heritage
or develop as she should…

CISSY/ ALL
Pretty Brown Gal…

JO
Sho ain't no place for the beaded and
bangled [bejeweled] female
who adorns herself more gaining grace,
To be lowered to her hands and knees
to scrub the floors of another's place.

CISSY/ ALL
Pretty Brown Gal…

JO
If you say it's a place for healthy-hipped
treasures

To walk in their natural sway,

Without being bothered by "psst, say girl"

Then I will go my way.

CISSY/ ALL

Pretty Brown Gal...

BUBU

Our "Sapphire's" and our "Ruby's"

have names that just don't rate

Cause we be surrounded by tricky white lies

 turned to myths and then self hate.

CISSY/ ALL

Pretty Brown Gal...

CELESTE

Ain't no place for the lioness

who raised children as the family's core

To work everyday for a living,

making child raising a chore.

CISSY
Pretty Brown Gal...

CISSY
Pretty Brown Gal...

CELESTE
Gotta make this a place for **Brown Gal**
Princesses
just like you and me.
Gotta steep in young black Nubian beings
(kings and queens)
their own point of dignity.

CISSY
Pretty Brown Gal...

BUBU
I owe it to my Mother and my Father
whose legacy supports this earth,
To build and dream and build and dream
  until their off-springs come first.

But right now,

Pretty Brown Gal...

This ain't no place for a Brown Gal

Princess.

(an African Princess).

CISSY

(innocently defiant)

Where's my **Pretty Brown Gal**...?

Here's that **Pretty Brown Gal**?

(pointing to herself)

Where's my **Pretty Brown Gal**...?

(pointing to OTHERS)

ALL

(indicating themselves)

Here's that **Pretty Brown Gal**! ! !

IV. <u>THE HATS</u>

EVE

(in the mirror/ becoming the mirror…
trying on hats—fedora and wide brim
church hat.)
I know why some black men
Call each other "man"   [niggah/ son/
dawg].
I mean, I know they use it as an ego-
boosting,
Kinship claiming name
That dilutes the strength
Of white folks' ego-busting ,
Manhood   denying   name   of   "boy"
[niggah/ son/ dawg].

*(**EVE** tosses **JO** the masculine hat)*

But I am a Black woman…
ego-needing, nation bearing WOMAN.

And I wish some Black men

Would forget their egos long enough

Not to call me "man" [niggah/ son/
dawg]

*(EVE hands **CELESTE** the feminine hat)*

*[**JO** and **CELESTE** mirror each other*

modeling their hats;

***CELESTE** feminine—**JO** masculine]*

JO

Yo mama,

Fine, foxy thang standing here before me.

You sho' looks mighty good I see.

CELESTE

Why thanks,

But what I know of you and this world,

I bet you say that to all the girls.

JO

Aw-w-w-w-w-w- baby,

Believe me. This ain't no line.

I only say it to the ones who are truly fine.

CELESTE

Uh huh,

I think I understand.

You're filling the role of a macho man.

JO

Macho wha' ?!

Naw sweetness. Naw not me.

I just like everything I see.

CELESTE

Well,

You've seen me a thousand times before.

And I don't always get this rap that's a bore.

JO

Yo, mama!

But cha' knows I loves ya..

And that's worth something on the market, I
bet cha'.

CELESTE
You think
I can trade it for some fine cuisine?
Or maybe a ride in a long limousine?

JO
Naw, shugah,
It won't get you all that.
But then you got me and my fine hat.

CELESTE
You know,
Now that you mention that hat of yours,
It's when you wear it that you start your
chorus.

JO
Say wha'?
A chorus you call it pet.

That's like music at the New York Met.

CELESTE

Hardly music

My mannish young thing.

Take off that hat! Scared you'll have a ring?

JO

Ring? Ring?

Do I hear bells inside my head?

Or is you hinting at fingers instead?

CELESTE

Hinting? Me?

You got me all wrong.

When it comes to marriage, I sing the whole
song.

JO

Yo mama!

But cha knows I loves ya..

And that's worth something on the market I
bet cha.

CELESTE

You know ,

You say that all the time.

To me and how many other girls in line.

JO

Now darlin',

What cha' wanna go and say that for?

You know you're the only one my heart
beats for.

CELESTE

No, my "man" [niggah/ son/ dawg]

It just dawns on me that

You only talk that way when you wear that
hat (like that)!

JO

My hat, brown shugah,

Is just an adornment.

It serves my character some serious compliment.

CELESTE

Character?

Compliment?

Honey, when you wear that hat you think you are God-sent.

JO

Now wait, baby cakes!

Who brought God into this?

But when He tossed out this hat, I don't think He missed.

CELESTE

God... He?

That's macho to a tee

For all you know, God might be a SHE.

JO

Yo, angel breath.

Now you've gone too far.

First you talked about my hat, now you giving God a scar.

CELESTE

Yeah? … Well,

There is one thing in the back of my head.

"We're all created equal." That's what SHE said.

JO

Well precious!

If we were all created equal we would have the same hat.

But you've got yours. Now what 'cha think about that?

CELESTE

Hmmmmmm!

I think it's pretty sad if the hat makes the "man" *[niggah/ son/ dawg].*

Without the hat, there's no reason for a Master Plan!?!

JO

So yo, doll face.

Don't question Divine Inspiration.

Just move yo' fine self over here in my direction.

[In moving to hug each other, they knock off each other's hat]

JO

(trying to hide his head)

Look out sweetheart!

You've bared me to the world.

Now everyone will see that I don't even have no curls.

CELESTE

(Snatching the masculine hat)

Ah ha!

Now let me see this crowning topper

And check out what makes it such a show stopper.

JO
Chocolate chip,
What cha' wanna go and do that for?
You think my hat is gonna make you a star?

CELESTE
Hmmmmmmmm!
I must admit this hat has a feel.
(CELESTE puts on JO's hat)
Here you try mine and see how it feels.
(CELESTE puts her hat on JO)

[They assume the personality if the other's hat—role reversal]

CELESTE
Yo daddy!
This brim is quite bad.

I see it's more than a sky piece or a mere
fad.

JO

Well dear.

This hat of yours is darling indeed.

Excuse me a second. I feel a sneeze.

CELESTE

Yo stuff!

Just blow the other way.

This hat is on me now and I intend for it to
stay.

JO

You… you

You can be so cruel in the things you say.

You'll regret talking to me this way.

CELESTE

Yo daddy!

But cha' knows I loves ya'!

And that's worth something on the market, I
bet cha'!

JO
Huh...
I guess you think I'm in no way wise.
I bet 'cha tell that to all the girls-- I mean,
guys.

*[JO and CELESTE discard hats and resume
their own identities.]*

V. CAUTION

[CELESTE   perfumes   herself—the scenting ritual]

BUBU

*(Mirrors **JO** with hat)*

He still fucks white girls

As if my un-willing blend was not enough—

He still fucks...

As if enough black boys had not lost their

stuff because of it—

He still fucks...

No matter that the black babies he sired are

growing up gut-bucked—

He still fucks...

Even though there is not enough Black male

"stuff "

To satisfy Black female "fluff"—

He still fucks

 white girls!!

And tells me not to waste my anger

On his unconscious danger

As he fucks…

 white girls.

So, I will go my way

and do my share

To help others raise his off-spring.

But with all I know

about myself and my past story,

I can't get over the gory

details of him…

Still fucking white girls.

(Puts hat away)

EVE

*(becomes a clock with **BUBU** and **JO** moving counter-clockwise—a time bomb of sorts)*

It's funny how time passes.

I mean without you even noticing—

*(**CISSY** sneaks and plays with "mama's" make up)*

Seconds turn into minutes…

Minutes into hours…

Hours to days…

Days to weeks…

Weeks, months…

Months, years

And people turn old and gray—

(CISSY freezes; clock freezes looking at her)

Right before your eyes.

As you perceive time—

Important or unimportant—

It passes on.

And it does bring about change.

CISSY

(CISSY plays with make-up and gets progressively serious;

CELESTE applies it seriously)

I learned that I wanted to be more

Than a carbon copy of my mother.

And I love my Mother!

She is the most supreme woman in my life.

But I wanted to develop

those things in me

That I did not inherit from her.

Not to love her less...

But to love myself more.

CELESTE

(reading newspaper)

They found 17,000 little bundles of joy—

unborn—

and packed in plastic containers

like potato salad,

stacked neatly inside a dempsey dumpster...

ready for disposal or scientific dabbling

depending on who repossessed

the dumpster first.

The figures are awesome

if my "guess-timate" math serves me well.

17,000 in one city in California...

(CISSY becomes a delegate and beckons CELESTE inside)

probably means 17,000 in one city in New York...

(BUBU becomes a delegate and beckons CELESTE inside)

means 17,000 in one city in Illinois...

(JO becomes delegate and beckons CELESTE inside)

means 17,000 in one city in Pennsylvania

(EVE becomes a delegate and beckons CELESTE inside)

Means 17,000 in one city in Texas

Means 17,000 in one city like D.C...

(CELESTE enters circle)

that's over 100,000

 and counting...

Thousands more in cities in between...

In one year.

The pitter- patter of those little feet
will not be heard.
The contributions of those tiny hands
will not be felt...
For they dangle limp
at the end of clipped umbilical rope.

That ain't about our BODIES ladies.

We talk about slavery
and how black people were deemed disposable
By the powers that ruled them.
We talk about the "holy-cost"
and how Jews were deemed disposable
By the powers that ruled them.
Who will talk about the babies deemed disposable
By the powers that rule them?

They can't sit-in.
They can't picket.

They can't protest.

They can't go on strike

They can't flee from persecution.

They can't scream...

STOP!!!

STOP KILLING ME!!!

One million per year,

If my guess-timate" math serves me well.

Contraception is one thing—

But this ain't about **our** bodies, ladies.

When will we,

and this includes me...

When will we learn to be free enough

to praise our names?!

When will we learn to worship ourselves

within our temples?!

When will we learn to be care-full enough

to select what enters it,

And once **we have selected** and allowed

entrance,

We worship the consequences?!

[I'm not talking about

Male imposed

violence…

or Rape …

Or incest…]

See, that ain't about our BODIES, ladies!

That's about our MINDS!

We have the strength to change HIS-story

We have the wisdom to enhance HER-story.

We have done it before.

We can do it again…

When we teach value to OUR feminine…

When we cherish OUR feminine devine.

We have done it before.

We can do it again…

When we stop destroying OURselves/ futures.

See, This ain't about our BODIES, ladies!
This ain't about our BABIES!
Naw, this ain't about our BODIES, ladies!
This is about **OUR MINDS**! ! !

JO

(becomes a farmer with the others)
Guard your seeds my brothers!
They are drops of gold.
The injection process
is only part of the way
 to sow Precious fruit
that will turn bitter on you
if planted in the wrong places.

Watch the ground you cultivate—
pushing apart ledges of unbaked sand.
The brown earth calls
 for pushing and pulling
in an effort to multiply rich creations
that manifest themselves
in the virtue of the earth.

Guard you seeds, my brothers!

Lest one who has none

Take them from you—

voluntarily.

And plant them

in artificial vineyards

to grow vines you will not recognize...

Vines that will grow

to entwine your throat and mine

in a clutch that will end in a barren song.

Guard your seeds, my bothers! ! !

BUBU

*(becomes a soldier at attention; progresses
into a march)*

Brothers... and Sisters!

Please be advised...

That the white man and the white woman—

(palms out—hands over eyes)

As we know them—

Are in their last days and times!

Be advised …

That the reason for cloning,

Sperm banking,

Inseminating, and bionics…(*animatedly*)

Is that "they" can no longer

 match us

child for child.

CISSY

(*marching*)

The baby battle is getting darker.

Look around you!

We are everywhere—

And there in numbers.

The 1990 [1980 / 2000/ 2010] census

counted us

And those of us who will have to go

To maintain the present balance of power.

So….

ALL

(marching)

We will experience famine

and wars

And un-natural epidemics—

Like sickle cell anemia,

cancer

Drug addiction and

Rap music

Gang wars

and

    A. -I. -D. -S. ....(letters pronounced as a
    drill cheer)

CISSY

That will cause death

to us

And to our children.

BUBU

Brothers and Sisters,

Please be advised...

JO

That all amounts of protection

Cannot be enough.

We can start by electing,

Appointing,

And then protecting

Our leaders.

Look at Martin Luther King, Jr.,

Angela Davis,

Idi Amin,

Winnie Mandela,

Nelson Mandela,

Malcolm X,

Steven Biko,

Chappy James,

Eldridge Cleaver—

All "discontinued"

Or discredited

For one of "their" reasons or another.

Look at Jesse Jackson,

Al Sharpton,

Lenora Fulani,

Leonard Jeffries,

David Dinkins,

Andrew Young,

Julian Bond,

Maxine Waters...

Kofi Anon...

We must be the ones

To hold them accountable.

And we must be the ones

 to hold court on them—

should court need to be held.

But we MUST do it—

WE must be the ones!!!

BUBU

Please be advised...

EVE

That the old trick

Of "divide and conquer"

Still works

As well as it used to.

If they can turn

Continent against continent,

Male against female,

Friend against friend,

Brother against sister,

Mother against child,

They can keep us from uniting.

They can keep us from reproducing.

BUBU

(moves like robot in "Lost in Space")
Warning!!! Warning !!! Warning !!!

CELESTE

(becomes a classroom teacher)
We must become responsible

for the education of our children

and the training *and employment* of our
peers.

We can teach and train in

Our homes,

Our churches,

Our community centers,

Our street corners,

Our bars, and

Our soul food restaurants.

(Each one assumes the activity of each location)

We have enough knowledge

In black communities around this country

And around the world,

To handle—

 and handle well --

All the survival stations we need.

We can no longer afford

Technological exclusivity.

BUBU

Hear me out!

The unemployment problems,

The Middle East problems,

The transportation and gas problems…

Are all manufactured problems

That affect black pockets

And that effects black numbers.

ALL

Brothers and Sisters!

JO

I urge you to be strong

In the face of these adversities.

EVE

I urge you to think

As "Brer Rabbit" *(in the briar patch)* would think

At a time like this.

CISSY

Let's take hold of our children!

CELESTE

Let us take hold of our families!

BUBU

Let us take hold of our story

And plan for the day

When we will govern our selves...

When we will govern <u>our</u> land!

ALL

Brothers and Sisters,

Please be advised...

BUBU

That the white man and the white woman—

(*palms out—hands over eyes*)

As we know them—

Are in their last days and times.

ALL

Let us prepare to rule... *ourselves!*

Let us prepare to rule our land!

Let us prepare to rule our destiny(ies)!

ALL

Chant with me….

(song)

I said work with me,

grow with me,

believe in me,

I said love with me

And **WE**

Can change the world…

MYO!

(button song with hummmmmmmm)

[The Original words of this song are:

God said work with me,

Grow with me,

Believe in me.

God said love with me

And we can change the world.

*** I am now Nichiren Shoshu Buddhist]

VI. TV

ALL
(an orchestra of distorted sounds; strobe
distortion…
distortion…
Miss- Representation
(Hands over breast like "Miss America"
sash ribbons)

JO
Distorted

EVE
Distended

CISSY
Bended

CELESTE
And twisted out of shape.

ALL

That ain't me on TV!

(hands frame face with "coon" grins.)

CELESTE

(Forming TV screen with EVE, JO becomes
maid/porter. CISSY says "Hi Ma")

That ain't my walk.

That ain't my talk.

Ain't too much of that mine.

It looks like me—sure...

Same color...

Same form....

But it has somehow been...

ALL

Distorted!

(hands frame face with goofy grins.)

EVE

Even though this "state of the art"
equipment
Is capable of traveling to and darn near
through
The rings that circle Saturn,
And get close enough to tell me
They are some kind of gas...

CISSY

It still distorts my ass...
(she cups her mouth like oops; the others
look at her admonishingly)
and makes me look like
something I don't even like.
And I like me.
I love me.
I love black people.
But I don't love what I see
When I see me on TV

ALL
Distorted!

(hands frame face with guns and/or being arrested.)

JO
So if the camera shows
What the camera knows—
It's not the camera that distorts.
(ALL freeze. CELESTE exits circle)

CELESTE
Then where,
Tell me …
Where does this distortion come from? ? ?

ALL
Distortion….
Distortion…
Miss—representation…
(Hands over breast like "Miss America" sash ribbons)

JO

Distorted…

EVE

Distended…

CELESTE

Bended…

ALL

And twisted out of shape.

*Is that **ME** on TV ? ! ?*

*[*That ain't me on TV!!!]

(frame faces with "coon" grin)

\- SHARP BLACK OUT-

MID-LOGUE

ALL

Daydreaming and I'm thinking of you…

Daydreaming and I'm thinking of you…

Daydreaming and I'm thinking of you…

Look at my mind—

Blowing away…

VII. <u>FOREPLAY</u>

EVE

(In the "Supreme-esque"position. CELESTE
paints her nails; the others let their hair
down)
Really, I'm like any other woman.
I bleed.
I need.
I laugh.
I cry.
I love.
And I long for loving too.

CISSY

(removes flower from her hair and plays
"love me... love me not" with petals)
I won't say "I love you."
But I do love loving you.
And you love loving me
Without saying "I love you."
So in some ways I do…

So sue me!

But find grounds that neither of us share

As reasons for not saying "I love you."

You do me swell…

So hell … *(cups her mouth)*

Why blow it with accolades that dim with

wilting daisies.

I won't say "I love you"

But I do love loving you.

BUBU

(practicing on the back of her hand)

Sometimes when we kiss…

I feel the nectar of what must be heaven

Flowing like a fountain

From you to me

And through me back to you.

I feel like you must be giving me life

Or more life

Or a willingness to live

To receive another one of your kisses.

When we kiss,

As we sometimes do,

I close my eyes and stars burst forth

In my conscious mind

And lead me to a place of lightness

Where my body has no place and

Only my mind can focus on you.

And I don't want to open my eyes

Until our kiss is over

And I don't want our kiss to end.

We kiss and the ringing in my ears

Starts a vibration in my soul

That shakes or seems to shake

The very earth I'm standing on,

And I have my hands full

holding my ground...

And holding you.

Sometimes,

I just want to give it all up

And sit down

or lie down

kissing you

and not worry about the colors

that start colliding in my head.

Sometimes when we kiss,

I feel you deep, down inside me

Past my private parts

That have reached a passionate peak

Beyond physical love—

And you do make good love

Or you make me love good –

Whatever…

I don't care now

because I am into your kiss.

Sometimes when we kiss

I call your name inside your mouth

Where I know without a word

and without a doubt

That you hear me

And I hear you –

Calling me.

Sometimes…

Sometimes…

Sometimes when we kiss

I know it's me

Who's on your mind.

Sometimes…

Sometimes…

EVE

(lighting a scented candle)

I wanna be

what you wanted me to be

The first time you looked at me

The reason you looked at me

again.

VIII. LOVE

CELESTE

(bathing the outline of her/ JO's aura)

Love me full and right and long

Cause I long for it

And you to come inside

And set up residence.

JO

(stroking the outline of CELESTE 'S aura)

Replace my vacant sign with your occupied

one

And make my insides your home.

Stoke gently the fire

And sit warm inside my love.

Come inside, my love.

Come.

CELESTE

Fill the echo of vacant places--

Hollow inside from discontent--

With your crevice-filling scream.

Let me call your name deep inside

The eardrum of your heart…

(BUBU joins them)

And hear you call me inside mine.

Come.

(CISSY joins them)

Bring forth an abundance

of spring water

that springs forth

life everlasting.

Come.

Set asunder the timber that braces

The inside of my soul.

Come

Come.

JO

Come.

Set asunder the timber that braces

The inside of my soul.

(EVE joins them)

Come.

Come inside a paradise

That lies just beyond other searching

fingertips.

(ALL create the heartbeat)

CELESTE & JO

Come....

Come...

CELESTE

Come deeper inside my insides

Because that's where I want you

And you want to be there too.

Come...

Come...

Come...

JO

Is it there?

(Indicating center of circle)

CELESTE

Is it there?

I piercingly ask you with my eyes…

JO

Just as piercingly you say no.

So plunge your insides

Deeper inside mine.

Come…

And be the thumping thrust I need you to be

Cause you are the thumping thrust I need.

Come…

(They begin the counter dance with each
other)

CELESTE

Come…

Let me beat the rhythm

Of a native drum song

You can feel deep inside your soul.

Come…

Come…

Come up…

JO

Come down…

In…

CELESTE

Out…

Of my longing passions.

Come…

JO & CELESTE

Come…

Come…

CELESTE

All over my popping senses

And make me aware that you are there

Moving your belongings inside.

JO & CELESTE

Come…

JO

Because you are willing to assume the rights

Of loving me right…

CELESTE

And wanting to come

Because you feel I want to

love you right.

CELESTE & JO

Come…

Come…

Deep inside.

JO

Come with the idea of settling

And expanding the existing structure.

CELESTE

Come with plans for a future together
Whether we come for past memories.

CELESTE & JO

Come!

JO

(removing top/which is also CELESTE
removing top)
Come my pet,
And tame the wild hairs on a head
That would not bow for many
But will bow for you
Because you asked me to…
Inside a way I understand.

CELESTE & JO

Come!

CELESTE

(removing her top)

Come…
And make it hard
For me
To say no more.
Love me!

JO
Love you!
Love me!

CELESTE
Love you!
Come…

CELESTE & JO
Love me…
Love you…
Come… come…
Ah-h-h-h-h-h-h-h-!!!!
Come… come…
Love come…
You come…

Me come…

You…

Me…

We…

We come…

We come…

Come!!!

Ah-h-h-h-h-h-h-h-h-h-h-h-h-h-h!!!!!

Love come through us…

(CELESTE enters circle as JO mimes

pulling. They minuet)

Come seal us…

Come…Come…

Come…

Ah-h-h-h-h-h-h-h-h—h-h-h-h-h-h-h-h-h-h-

h-h-h!!!!!!!!

CELESTE

Oh love…

JO

My love…

CELESTE & JO

(fall spent, to the floor)

So glad you came
inside.

JO

Please….

CELESTE

Please…

CELESTE & JO

Please…
Come again ! ! !

IX.   <u>CIGARETTE</u>

*(**ALL** puffs on and exhales "cigarette")*
CISSY
(with child-like gestures)
I'm gonna tell it on you-u-u-…
I'm gonna tell it on you-u-u-u….
I'm gonna tell it on you-u-u-u-u-u--!

BUBU
Niggah had another
And the other niggah lowered my ratings.
I stood number 2 on a "top two" survey
And nothing I did changed my niggah's
mind.

Niggah had another
And I was the other niggah
in the way.
Fly away.
Get it All.
Make it good.

Cause it won't last.

See, the other niggah

Is only getting a little piece

Of a well baked pie

I made special for myself.

Niggah had another…

CISSY

(softly)

I'm gonna tell it on you…

X. SEPARATION

JO

I'm sorry,
 but I can't promise I'll always be here…
by your side
holding your hand
sharing your joy and sorrow.
I can't promise that life with me
Will be a haven,
Or we'll have all the things we want
Or all of our plans will go perfectly.
Nor can I promise that my friends will be
yours.
There is no guarantee that yours will be
mine,
Or that our families will always agree.
I can't promise that I will always be the
same me,
Never growing older or younger—
Or that my ideals and morals will never
change.

I can't promise I will always love you
 as strongly or as deeply as I do now…

But I can promise that
While I'm here, I'll hold your hand
*(reaches towards **CELESTE**)*
And share your trials and triumphs.
While we are together,
*(reaches toward **EVE**)*
I will give you all I can
And work like a mad fool to make our
dreams come true.
I will accept you for you
(reaches toward BUBU)
Regardless of our friends and family.

Certainly I'll grow older
But I'll cling desperately
To the things proven true
In my youth.
(almost to self)
And having loved you,

I promise
 that as long as I live and breathe,
A part of you will be with me
And a piece of my heart will always be
yours.
I'm sorry…
*(turns away and assumes the fencing
position)*

EVE
*(from fencing position begins to "air fence"
toward JO)*
And yet a "piece" became so precious
That you pieced me apart
And tore at my heart
When I told you all along that I cared.
Things I asked you not to do
Became the things you tried to
Use against me in the end.
I told you of my desires
And how you could quench my fires
And you blew empty the other way.

You said I made you choose
Between your friends and who's
Been sharing your dreams--
sharing YOUR dreams--
All these years.

Well after all your lies
I just could not hide
The fool you were
And the fool you'd made of me.
Yet, when all my tears were cried
I had to realize
that love had found me
and left me wise.
*(touche' and back to fencing position,
dropping "sword")*

EVE & CELESTE
(song)
Some things you never get used to…
no never, not ever.
Some things you can't get over

no way… no way.

CELESTE

Just look, when you left

You took the sunshine from my sky

And I…

could barely live with the gloom.

When you left,

You took the happiness from my heart

And left me here with no room to get over

you.

ALL

Some things you never get used to

No never … not ever…

Some things you can't get over

No way… now ay…

CELESTE

I thought I'd cry until my eyes were empty

And I had no more tears.

I thought I'd hide my lonely face from the

world

Who had known us all those years,
 until I got over you.

ALL

Some things you never get used to—

No never … not ever…

Some things you can't get over

No way… no way…

CELESTE

I know I'll live to sing a new song

Inside my soul—where I had space only for

you.

But make no mistake,

You'll always live here in my heart.

And when I feel love, I will remember you.

(heartbeat and bathe JO's aura outline)

ALL

Some things you never get used to—

No never … not ever…

Some things you can't get over—

No way…

No way…

No way…

XI. DREAM

EVE

Sleep…

Sleep…

Sleep…

(putting the others to sleep[using bubbles])

deep sleep…

JO

(tries to shrug it off)

Come, blessed sleep.

With your soothing, easing, healing powers.

Wash away the bitter taste that comes from

eating "humble pie"

When you'd rather have food instead.

(sleeps)

BUBU

(fighting it off)

Blow away the stink of garbage

and fuming industry

and messed up sewage

that always seems to surround

black communities.

Blot out all the colors—

Red, blue, green—

And the two that people see most often

And try to judge you by.

(sleeps)

CELESTE

(yawning)

Sleep,

overcome the chirp of crickets

That seeps through the flimsy walls

And screen-less windows of [some of]our

house(s).

Overcome the quietness

Of having the gas and electricity turned off

Cause we couldn't pay the bills. (*sleeps)*

CISSY

(stretching)

Sleep, ease the ache in my father's back

Erase the furrows in my mother's brow,

Pacify the hurt in my heart

From realizing that I'm black like them

And work will come harder for me also.

(goes to sleep)

EVE

So sleep.

Blessed sleep…

Overtake them(us) …. and make them(us)

….

If not eager—

Able—to live tomorrow….

Sleep…

Sleep…

Deep sleep…

CISSY

(EVE waves CISSY into her dream-trance)

Lost child!

Lost child!!

Lost child!!!

Have you seen her?

Heard her?

Felt her…

Anywhere in your heart? (*heartbeat*)

Lost child!

Gone since Friday –

A long weekend for some…

Vacation time for others.

Twilight time for a lost child

Without her dinner

And without her mother.

Lost child!

Lost to ignorance…

Lost to arrogance

Lost to greed….

lost to poverty....
lost to sentiment...
lost to society...
lost her virtue...
lost to herself...
lost to God/*dess*—
  it seems!
Lost child!

Have you seen her?
Please call somebody
(use "Aunt Sarah's phone)
at some number...
somewhere...
who cares.

Phone number gone.
Covered with graffiti
(spray paint L-O-S-T !)
Of a "graffi-tic" society
Bent on doing "graffi-tic" things
Since they paint moustaches

On lost children's faces

And would not call if they had seen her

For they had not felt her in their hearts.

Lost child!

Have you seen her?

(mocking in the voice of an unconcerned

"mannered" woman)

"It's not me. It's not mine.

 Not that I don't care,

It's just that there are so many lost children

everywhere

that concern for this one is hard."

Lost child!

"Lost child? Lost child, you say…

Lost child where?

I don't see anyone."

(CISSY goes back to sleep)

JO

(EVE waves JO into dream-trance: JO gets
"high" on several drugs)
They got me high on "stuff" one night
and I nodded into another world.
It was a world that fought for truce on
wars…
That was "colorful" instead of black and
white…
That allowed women to develop—
And men-- not so much..

It was a world
That let short people walk tall…
That let "southpaws" go north…
That "abled" the disabled…
That allowed gays "gaiety"…
That repainted "blue" for girls"…
And repainted "pink" for boys"…
That "re-roled" sex…
 That cleaned up the filth…
That freaked out the drugs….
That dried out the booze…

That made rich the poor…

That devalued the dollar…

That created music for listeners…

That created silence for listeners…

That made sacred *themselves* …

Then I came down…

And so did that world.

(JO goes back to sleep)

BUBU

(EVE waves BUBU into her dream-trance)

I will live to beat my drum again.

I will…

I will!

I will live to beat my drum again

And tell my children their story

 in a language they will understand.

I will live!

I will live to see

the picture of the world

Painted darker—

It's truer hue—

With a realization and admiration

That me and my people lived here too.

I will live!

I will live to hear

the story of so many

who have lived before me.

And I will capture it

And capsule it

 And send it

Careening through time and space.

I must live!

I must live to connect the frayed edges

Of continents shorn by dulled scissors

In the hands of an insensitive cutter.

I will live!

I will live to beat…

I will live to beat my drum…

I will live to beat my drum again…

Again ! ! !

*(**BUBU** falls back asleep)*

CELESTE

(EVE waves CELESTE out of sleep-trance)

I saw the sun rise

Through a hazy, foggy mist

The morning of my birthday.

And because I was so anxious about that

birthday,

I thought that unshining morn

Was one of the most beautiful

I had ever seen.

That dawn

(ALL go to earlier birthday party)

Crowded my mind with memories

Of earlier birthdays…

And party-dressed friends…

And pin-the-tail

And gifts

And cards with dollars

And (twin) iced cakes…

And ice cream

And candles…

CISSY

Make a wish….

CELESTE

And not celebrating birthdays

(blows out scented candle)

And this birthday

And this unexplainable joy.

I know the coming year *is* going to be a

good one

Because *I am* positively looking forward to

it.

I know a new phase of woman-hood lies

ahead for me.

I am finally beginning to realize that

To grow older is inevitable…

To grow wiser is controllable…

To grow happy and peaceful is attainable.

EVE

(begins to reveal herself)

I am the Eve no one ever spoke of—

Dark—

Like the midnight hour.

I am the new woman,

The coming woman,

The first woman,

To think… to say… to do

Many of the things I have.

I am the new image of things hoped for.

*(places **CELESTE** in the center of **ALL**)*

I am the fresh vision of things to come.

I am the Eve no one ever spoke of.

Beyond Adam,

I have gone inside myself

*(Awakens **JO** and puts her next **to***

***CELESTE**, arm outstretched hand just*

above shoulder)

And discovered

12 ribs is all I need

to cage the blood…

the guts…

the rage…

I use daily

To be the Eve I am.

No one mentioned me.

Beyond the apple of sin and evil,

I have cored and developed

Goodness and beauty

In myself and in many other EVE's

Who dared to look inside their souls.

Who spoke of me?

Yet,

I am the Eve who nurtured nations

With a bosom full of wholesome nutrition

*(awakens **BUBU** and puts her to the side of*

***CELESTE** opposite **JO**, hand just above*

***CELESTE**'s shoulder)*

That civilizations of EVE's before me
perfected
And passed to me to perfect more
And pass on to young, starving EVE's
*(awakens **CISSY** and places her to the side*
*of **CELESTE**, hand just above shoulder)*
To perfect more and pass again.

I am the EVE no one ever dreamed of
And I'm darker now than the midnight hour.
*(takes her place next to **CELESTE**, hand*
just above shoulder)
I am the EVE no one ever spoke of—
I am the dawning of a brand new day! ! !
*(They all clasp **CELESTE**)*

EPILOGUE

(the uniting of personas continues)

CELESTE

That's right,

From nothing to something

I have learned to build…

ALL

The *body* of woman

We have become!

CELESTE

With fingertips and elbow grips

I've learned to add to what was there

And make something different.

ALL

BROWN GAL RISING… we [I] have

begun!

CELESTE

With dreams of friends

And fears of foes

And energy from places on "High",

I have taken time and relaxed my mind

And created something for worlds to see…

ALL
That's right!

CISSY
Emerging…

BUBU
Standing…

CELESTE
Needing…

JO
Demanding….

ALL

(hands lifted each word til they are at
CELESTE's head level)

BROWN GAL RISING...

that's me!!!

----- **FADE TO BLACK**-----

Images From Brown Gal's Rising

Theater 22, NY

Under 1 Roof, NY

Brooklyn College, NY

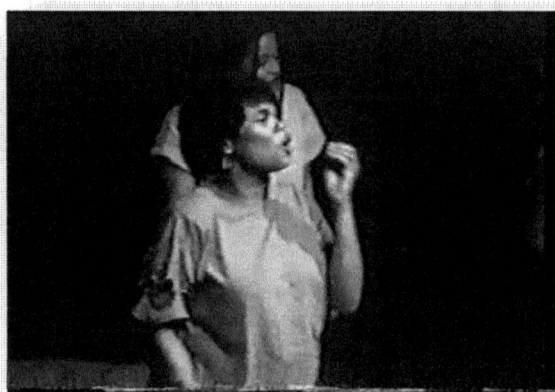

Author's Comments

BROWN GAL'S RISING is a life-full of poetry. And 20 years ago when I had the honor of presenting my work to a public audience, I had no idea the impact it would have on my and many other lives. But that is the nature of art—we cannot truly measure its influence, we just know it is present. BROWN GAL'S RISING "influenced" the early careers and lives of actors like Renee Joshua-Porter, Curtiss Cooke, Renee Flemings, Nicole Ari Parker, Cherise Trahan, Kathi Bentley, Robert Evans, Terry Wyche' (full casts listed in Acknowledgements).

So 20 years later, I want(ed) to honor our efforts again and the best way to do that, I felt, was to publish the book, BROWN GAL'S RISING. When I pulled all the archive material, I saw that I had VHS copies of all 3 Productions: The Maiden Voyage at Theatre 22, The Brooklyn College version, and the Under One Roof version, that experienced the great Phyllis Hyman on stage with the cast singing… (that is a bonus track that we are making available to a special few). So I "stilled" some shots from the videos to include here in the book.

But back to the life-full of poetry…I was born a brown-skinned twin to a fairer skinned brother, Cecil, (see picture) in Dallas, TX. I wrote poetry for as long as I can remember…little snatches of thoughts here and there. All those emotions that I

might not speak on, I wrote down—and I kept it private. I self-published my first book, "**JUST AS I AM**", which was a snack pack of poetry on personal perspectives. When my twin brother died through an unfortunate set of circumstances, I was totally devasted. The title of the poem "Somethings you Never get Used to..." was written essentially for him. The birthday references—twin iced cakes, the anxiety of not celebrating birthdays, and that BGR happens on a birthday is totally stimulated by my emotional catharses round my brother's loss. Then there was a play I did with Irma P. Hall that earned me my Actors Equity card in Dallas at Theatre Three. That play was Ntozake Shange's choreo-poem, "For Colored Girls Who Considered suicide, When the Rainbow is Enough", and it effectively changed the course of my life. I was officially a professional actress and this "choreo-poem" format offered a home for all those poems I had been writing.
I started putting all those poems together! I noticed that that they seemed to come from 5 different people-- but all those people were me. So I gave them names and acknowledged them as aspects of myself. While I was developing BROWN GAL'S RISING, my Mother Naomi Bruton, was diagnosed with and subsequently passed from breast cancer. I had just

copywritten BGR. Devastated again, I back-burnered BGR until the early 90's when Jeffrey Miller/Wayne Jelks and Blue Diamond Theatre Company offered me a production opportunity that spawned my Directorial career. I had tendered BGR to other directors but they did not see my vision.

By our first Production date in 1991, my younger brother, Ciscoe II, who had danced in 3 Broadway shows by the time he was 30, was in the end stages of A.I.D.S. [Why do they call it AIDS –it don't help nobody!] I was straddling between medicine and art...and again, devastated. The first production was postponed by several months because of funding. But I was kissed to still be able to get the original cast that I had auditioned. Renee Joshua-Porter was pregnant and thought I would not use her in the play but I did. And we both danced with joy; one, she is an incredible talent and two, Brown Gal Rising was having a baby!!!

Now I say all this to say, no matter how much I/you accomplish, how far I/you travel, how old I am/ you are, how much I/you overcome or how much I/you support others through their "stuff", as Women of Color, sooner or later in the

course of conversation or relationship
I/you will be called "gal"...

This "GAL" decided to embrace the
process of my life ...and embrace the
term... and move forward with my
Feminine Divine-- rising...which by
definition means to add value to; to
assume an elevated position from a lower
one—to get up!!!
I Rise! Join me...

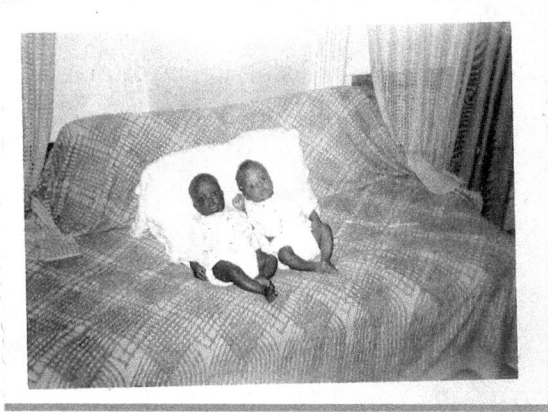

About Cecelia Antoinette

Just call me CECE—is a Dallas "boomed", NYC groomed, LA blooming actress who has appeared on Broadway in Lincoln Center Theatre's MULE BONE and in numerous off-Broadway, Regional and International theatres.

*** On TV, Cece has appeared on MAD MEN, GIRL FRIENDS, DESPERATE HOUSEWIVES, BROTHERS & SISTERS, CROSSING JORDAN, LAW & ORDER: SVU, WANTED, THE OFFICE, SEX & THE CITY, THE CHRIS ROCK SHOW,

JIMMY KIMMEL LIVE!, THE RICKI
LAKE SHOW, and storytelling on A
PLACE OF OUR OWN.

***In films, she can be seen in the top rated
YES MAN starring Jim Carrey, DANCE FU
starring Kel Mitchell and directed by Cedric
The Entertainer, NJ DRIVE, BULLET TO
THE BRAIN, AFTER SCHOOL,
BEAUTIFUL THINGS, MOTV and
numerous independent films. She also
appears in several national and regional
commercials.

***Cece is currently touring
WATERMELON-GIT IT WHILE IT'S
HOT ! the historical and hysterical
rites-of-passage one-woman comedy about
growing from Negro girlhood into
empowered womanhood
in Hamilton Park – the first neighborhood
built "from the ground up for colored
families" in Dallas, TX. She also performs
THE AWE SERIES – Vignettes of African

& African American Women of Endeavors in libraries and arenas around the country. ***As an MC Extraordinaire she was one of the first female Guest Host of Amateur Night at the APOLLO. She is the Founder/Artistic Director of MOSAIC JEWELS –THE GEMS OF COMEDY— taking funny to a whole new dimension (diverse female sketch and stand-up).

***As a Director, CECELIA is a member of The Women's Project Directors' Forum, the Frank Silvera Writer's Workshop Directors Pool and Lincoln Center Theatre's Directors' Lab.

***As a writer and Spoken Word Artist, CECE has published and produced works "BROWN GAL'S RISING", "JUST AS I AM" and "JUKEBOX POETRY" to public and critical acclaim. She loves to "edu-tain" children of all ages as a Teaching Artist and as KOO KOO the Klown. She tekes "The

World Is OUR Stage" as a Theatre
workshop to schools and libraries.

Actress/ Producer

Founding Artistic Director

PLUMEings Productions

November 1984 – Present

PLUMEings Productions

produces, promotes, performs

dazzling artistic expressions !!!

With emphasis on Women and Peoples of Color

CeCelia Antoinette: TV/ Film (to date)
**my Wish List Show, Series Regular

WEEDS

2 BROKE GIRLS

SWITCHED AT BIRTH

VICTORIOUS

MAD MEN,

GIRL FRIENDS,

DESPERATE HOUSEWIVES,

BROTHERS & SISTERS,

CROSSING JORDAN,

LAW & ORDER: SVU,

WANTED,

THE OFFICE,

SEX & THE CITY,

THE CHRIS ROCK SHOW,

JIMMY KIMMEL LIVE!,

THE RICKI LAKE SHOW,

SHOWTIME AT THE APOLLO

PBS, A PLACE OF OUR OWN.

YES MAN starring Jim Carrey,

DANCE FU, starring Kel Mitchell and directed by Cedric
The Entertainer,

NJ DRIVE,

AFTER SCHOOL,

BULLET TO THE BRAIN,

BEAUTIFUL THINGS,

MOTV

As always, to Mama. . .

A Photo Mosaic Tribute to
Phyllis Hyman